B. Raulsen

The Art of Taste

A Gourmet Guide
to Vegetarian Cooking

Beatrix Rohlsen

GOURMET CREATIONS
SANTA BARBARA

Cover design, book design, typography and image scanning
by Frank Goad, Santa Barbara, California

Color film by Grayphics, Santa Barbara, California

Printed by Printworks, Van Nuys, California

Cover illustration by the author: *Full Moon Invitation,* 1993, watercolor on paper

Author photo by Nicola Dill, Pacific Palisades, California

LIBRARY OF CONGRESS CATALOG CARD NUMBER: 94-96526

ISBN 0-9643302-0-2

GOURMET CREATIONS
Post Office Box 41136
Santa Barbara, California 93140

To the spirit of Esalen & White Lotus

CONTENTS

Foreword..13

Acknowledgements 15

What You Need to Know Before Cooking......17

Shopping and Ingredients............................18

Helpful Hints...18

Introduction...21

SOUPS

Tomato Basil Soup.......................................28

Thai Red Lentil Soup...................................29

German Erbsensuppe 30

Carrot Cream Soup 30

Carrot Zucchini Soup..................................31

Mixed Vegetable Soup a la Ron 32

Pumpkin Yam Soup.....................................33

Potato Leek Soup 33

Garden Potpourri 34

Miso Vegetable Soup 34

Lentil Soup..35

Chili con Tofu 36

Spinach Soup 37

SALADS

Curry-Rice Salad 42

Steamed Vegetable Salad 42

Spinach-Yam Salad......................................43

Green Bean-Mushroom Salad 44

SALADS (continued)

Spicy Garbanzos a la Morocco 44
Humus...45
German Beet Salad 45
Beet Apple Salad 46
Szechwan Soba Noodles..........................46
Spicy Black Bean Salad............................47
Wild Rice Salad 48
Seaweed Salad..48
Lentil Tabuli Salad 49
Raita..50

SALAD DRESSINGS

Dill Dressing 54
Orange Yam Dressing................................54
Avocado Cilantro Dressing 55
Tahini Carrot Dressing 55
Vinaigrette 56
Tofu Curry Dressing.................................56

SAUCES

Indonesian Peanut Sauce..........................57
Tofu Cilantro/Parsley Cream Sauce...........57
Mushroom Gravy.......................................57
Salsa 58
Guacamole 58
Tofu Sour Cream 59
Tofu Ricotta..59
Tofu Feta 60
Almond Mayonnaise 60
Tarragon Sauce...61
Almond Sauce 61
Sweet Sauces (Vanilla and Carob).............61

CHUTNEYS

Pear Orange Chutney. 65
Apple Lemon Chutney............................65
Pineapple Chutney 66

TOFUS

Scrambled Tofu 67
Marinated Baked Tofu Slices 68
Tofu Patties 68

BREAKFAST POTATOES

Potatoes au Gratin 71
Rosemary Potatoes 71
Potato Delight 72

ENTRÉES

Stir-Fry Vegetables with Baked Tofu 77
Middle Eastern Stuffed Zucchini 79
Lasagna 80
Polenta Spinach Pie................................82
Tarragon Vegetable Casserole 83
Lentil Potato Casserole 84
Pasta With Green Veggies........................84
Pesto 85
Pasta de Pomodore 86
Roasted Bell Pepper................................87
Nasi Goreng de Indonesia 87
Gado Gado Indonesia.............................88
Thai Curry..89
Enchilasagna/Enchiladas 90
Indian Curry...91
Mushroom Tempeh Stroganoff................92
Broccoli with Sesame 94

ENTRÉES (continued)

Rice Nut Loaf 94
Ginger Carrots 95

BREADS

Basic Yeast Dough 100
Sunflower Seed Bread 102
Multi-Grain Bread 102
Italian Oregano Bread 103
Onion Bread...103
Ingrid's Quick Bread 104
Cornbread...104
Raisin Bread 105

MUFFINS

Banana Muffins 109
Blueberry Muffins...................................110
Whole Wheat Bran Muffins...................110

PANCAKES & FRENCH TOAST

Oat-Buttermilk Pancakes 115
Banana Pancakes 116
Corn Quinoa Pancakes...........................116
French Toast 117

DESSERTS

Strawberries with Vanilla Sauce..............119
Banana Ice Cream 120
Nut Date Balls...120
Rice-Apricot Pudding.............................120
Mousse au Chocolat/Carob 121
Tofu-Strawberry Mousse........................121
Mango-Strawberry Mousse.....................122

Orange Pears with Chocolate Sauce 123

CAKES

Carrot Cake...125
Apple Walnut Cake.................................126
Heavenly Apricot Bars............................127
Peach Cobbler. 128
German Pflaumenkuchen.......................129
Tofu-Cheese Fig Cake 130

COOKIES

Brownies 131
Oat Chews 132
Ginger Snaps..132

MISCELLANEA

Sufi Story...137
Menu Ideas 139
Afterword...141

POEMS

Desert Rocks... 25
One Rose Affair...................................... 38
Let It Flow..51
Mountain Wind......................................62
Love 73
Life Wind...97
Menopause..107
Be 50...113
Wise Woman...134

PAINTINGS

Red Mountain Sky.................................. 23

Fire Dance 39
Landscape 63
Mystic Path 75
Ceremonial Dance 111
Red Flower 135

FOREWORD

BY TRACEY RICH

I FIRST MET BEATRIX as she emerged from the steamy sulfur springs of Esalen's hot baths. She was introduced to me by my husband as the new White Lotus cook! She says that she will never forget the look on my face. It was one of shock and conflict unsuccessfully covered by years of rearing in Southern politeness.

You know the phrase, "If it's not broken, don't fix it." Well, I had been trying for months to fix something that was broken and pretending that it was not. Beatrix saw on my face in the moment of our meeting not only the surprise that my husband Ganga had continued the search for a great cook unbeknownst to me, but a ray of hope mixed with fear of the unknown, months of training down the tubes, and the question of what to do with the broken cook back home. But I can happily say that I bless the day I met her.

I love to eat. I love to watch a master at work. I love that we have created a place of beauty where people can feel nurtured, get healthy and grow in every aspect of themselves. I love nature. I love people. I love poetry and passion. And for all of these reasons it is easy for me to love Beatrix. She is natural. She is beautiful and nurturing. Her work is masterful. She has poetry and passion in her soul. And, she can cook!

I used to joke that a Center such as ours needed not only a great cook (for my tastes run high), but that we needed a "shrink" in the kitchen. I say this because I have learned after years of cooking, being a waitress, and being a hostess, that people's true natures are revealed when hungry. When we created the White Lotus retreat we wanted it to be an extension of our home. A relaxed place where people could learn about Yoga, diet and lifestyle. In our house everyone congregates in the kitchen. We left the

Center kitchen open to the main gathering area for its elements of warmth and learning. Some cooks deplore this set-up. They cannot stand the interruptions, the scrutiny, the traffic or the growling stomachs. Beatrix, on the other hand, loves it, and even on a bad day handles it with grace and equanimity. I have seen her years of training as a social worker, school teacher, Reichian therapist and gourmet cook challenged in our kitchen.

Beatrix is a wonderful teacher. She teaches through her exquisite food. She teaches through her focus. To watch her kneading dough is to watch the meditation of the Zen master. She is earthy; at the same time she flows like water. Whether she alters a friend's recipe or creates one out of the ethers, her touch transforms. When she cooks we are fed on many levels.

The recipes in this book will not only be a creative journey when we prepare them, but knowing Beatrix as I do, I know they are her gift to us. They have been long awaited. May they always be celebrated.

ACKNOWLEDGEMENTS

W HEN I THINK ABOUT who got me started to write this book, my father comes to my mind. From him I learned to take risks and also to be responsible for what I want and to follow through. As a child I often did not understand why I should be responsible for my life; today I really value this teaching he gave to me. Tracey Rich and Ganga White, Directors of the White Lotus Foundation, opened their Center and their hearts to me and gave me the opportunity to be creative with food. They encouraged me through their trust to expand my imagination of being a vegetarian cook. Without their support this book would not have been written. Devin Morgan was my biggest support in my weakest point, organizing all the technical details. She always knew a way to motivate me when I was ready to give up. Tiana Blackburn, my roommate, had to put up with me taking over the apartment with my computer. She was one of the first people who got to see the starting pages and her supportive feedback helped me to get over my doubts and insecurities. Martin Gewirtz, who got inspired by my recipes, helped me to get over my language barrier and straightened out my English. Alan Mello, through all my time cooking in Esalen, shared his professional knowledge as a chef with me. Janat Dundas, my artistic friend, was always available to discuss my writing and was open to painting experiences. She is a wonderful teacher. Wendy Miller, whom I met in Santa Barbara, supported me as friend and also gave me much of her professional knowledge as an editor. Nicola Dill, who popped into my life from the same city in Germany, speaking my language, provided me with the beautiful photograph for the book cover.

Above all, I am thanking Frank Goad for his expert guidance and for all the time he spent to create the final book.

There are many friends more who supported me, and everybody in their own unique way. My thanks to all of them, and of course to all the people who have eaten my food, encouraging me to write a book. Without them this book would not have happened.

What You Need to Know Before Cooking

• All recipes are for 4-6 people, if it does not say differently.

• The temperature for the baking oven is mostly 375°F.

• If I don't specify the oil, then I use canola oil. Canola oil is the best for sautéing.

• There are three different kinds of recipes throughout the book:
    exact measurements
    rough measurements
    no measurements

• Remember that it is easy to add spices to a dish you are preparing, but it is difficult to take them out. Be gentle with seasonings and always taste before you put more in.

• GHEE is clarified butter and does not burn when heated.

• SWEETENERS are honey, maple syrup or apple juice.

• ARROWROOT is a starch and can be used as egg replacer. 1/3 cup water and 1/3 tablespoon arrowroot equals one egg.

• TOFU: *Soft tofu* is used for creams, sauces and mousses. *Firm tofu* is used for fillings, scrambled tofu, patties and feta.

• LEMON GRASS is used in Thai cooking. It is available, fresh, in most oriental or farmers' markets.

• KOMBU is a dried seaweed available in oriental markets.

• All recipes in this book can be changed, so that they get your touch. Take from them only what you need and ignore the rest. If you don't have an ingredient, leave it out or replace it with something similar.

• Allow yourself to create some meals that taste different than you thought they would. This is a way to find out what to change the next time.

• Now have a look at the shopping list and then you are ready to experiment. Enjoy what you are doing and everybody will like to eat your food.

Shopping and Ingredients

To make cooking easy and joyful, it would be good to have at home the ingredients which are used in these recipes. All the following ingredients can be bought in health food stores or oriental markets.

Arrowroot	*Carob Powder*	*Rice Vinegar*
Agar Agar	*Carob Chips*	*Sambal Olec*
Kuzu	*Soy Milk*	*Cumin Powder*
Nutritional Yeast	*Rice Dream*	*Sesame Oil*
Tahini	*Soba Buckwheat Noodles*	*Amazake*
Tamari	*Balsamic Vinegar*	

Helpful Hints

Throughout my time cooking at Big Sur's Esalen Institute and Santa Barbara's White Lotus Yoga Retreat Center, I learned many little tricks which made the preparation of meals so much easier that I am happy to share them with you.

• RICE: Rice has the tendency to get mushy. There are two things you can do to avoid that. After washing the rice, dry roast it in a pot. Stir frequently so that it won't burn. Than add cold water and bring to a boil in a covered pot. When it boils, stir it once, cover again and turn heat to very low. Do not uncover for 45 minutes. Looking into the pot before the rice is done is what makes it mushy.

• GARLIC: To peel garlic cloves easily, smash them a little with a small bottle or the flat side of a knife.

• BREAD: To heat up a loaf of bread, or rolls, or croissants—spray with cold water before putting into the baking oven. That gives them a crunchy outside.

• NUTRITIONAL YEAST: This is a great substitute for parmesan cheese when used in dishes such as pesto and pasta sauce.

• BAKING: If you are baking something and the top gets too brown too fast, cover it loosely with aluminum foil.

• SPICES: If you want to explore different spices or herbs and you are not sure what it will taste like, then take some of your dish out into a small bowl and then add the spice. If you like it, you can add it to the whole dish. Add spices always in little amounts at a time. It is easy to add more, but it is difficult to to take them out.

• POTS: If you have burned your stainless steel pot, cover the bottom with water, add baking soda (1 tablespoon up to 1/2 cup, depending on how big the bottom of the pot is) and boil it for 5-10 minutes. Then clean it right away.
    Cast iron pots and pans need to be heated up after being washed, and then oiled. It keeps them from rusting.

• LEGUMES: Do not add salt to legumes before they are done cooking. Salt closes the bean, so it takes much more time to cook them.

• ALUMINUM FOIL: Aluminum foil dissolves into baked food, especially when it touches tomato based foods. Cover your baking pan with parchment paper and then aluminum foil.

• PASTA: Add some oil to the pasta water to keep the pasta from sticking together.

• AVOCADOS: Drizzle lemon juice over opened avocados so they do not turn brown. Add an avocado pit to guacamole to keep it from turning brown.

• GHEE: Ghee is clarified butter. Heat one pound of butter on low heat. Let it melt completely. Turn heat to medium. With a spoon skim off the foam. When the butter starts to boil, turn down the heat and cook for about ten minutes more. Strain into a glass jar. Ghee keeps in the refrigerator for a long time. Makes about one cup.

INTRODUCTION

YOU MIGHT WONDER how Cooking and Art are related. Let me tell you a story. When I first came to the States seven years ago I decided to attend a Vipassana Meditation retreat at the Lama Foundation in New Mexico. For ten days I approached everything with an open mind and consciousness, and experienced food in ways I had never before seen or tasted.

Eating was no longer just a function to appease my hunger; it became a meditation. In being aware of what I was putting into my mouth, I could taste all the different flavors and textures in the food. I found myself enjoying the food much more than usual because I could see, taste and feel that this food had been prepared with a meditative mind and with love.

Through this experience, I realized how little I had cared when cooking for myself or for friends. It had never occurred to me that love could be a factor in the preparation of food and in how food would feel in my stomach. This way of preparing and eating food taught me that:

> *Meditation awakens my taste senses,*
> *Presentation feeds my creative eye and*
> *Love helps to digest the food.*

After only ten days of eating this way, I felt so much better in my body that I decided to try a different way of cooking for myself and for others.

It worked. All the resistance and frustration that I used to have when I had previously cooked suddenly changed. And, much to my surprise and delight, I found that it did not involve an increase in effort or time—just a change in my mind set. Since I began to cook with a meditative mind, an artistic eye and love, not only has my cooking improved, but my creativity has evolved as well. This way of cooking led me to painting and writing.

It has also helped me to use cookbooks in new and different ways. I never really liked the tedium of following recipes exactly, but I did not trust my eye or my own taste. We all know for example that spices are used in small amounts. So why does every recipe tell us to take 1 teaspoon of this and 1/2 teaspoon of that? It never made sense to me, but for years I followed the recipes exactly because I thought if I would change anything the result would be a disaster.

Now I know that this is not true, and I use cookbooks as an inspiration rather than as sacred texts.

Just imagine a painter opening a book on painting which tells him to take one brush stroke of red, then three brush strokes of blue and so on. When the painting is completed it is called *Red Mountain Sky*. It's a great painting, but it is not the painter's creation.

Wouldn't it be better for the painter to get an idea of his or her own about a red mountain sky? And that is what this cookbook is about. You get an idea, and then you create your own version—your own meal.

Relax and take your time to read this book, and enjoy doing it. You may be thinking: Who wants to relax when cooking is demanded? Don't we just want to get it over with, and then relax? That at least was my own experience for many years. Cooking was not really fun, it was something that I had to do.

That has changed for me. And I hope after you read this book, and you start to experiment with food, it will also change for you.

Enjoy what you are doing and your meal will be perfect.

$\sim$

Red Mountain Sky, 1993
Colored ink on paper

DESERT ROCKS

Brown—golden—green
Beautiful colors
melt together with the blue sky.
Rocks are talking to me,
laugh at me—smile at me.
They dance with the sky and
talk with the wind.
They feel close with blooming cactus
and know, they are different.
Big Jumbo Rock loves the difference.
Light and shadow play together.
Each important and equal strong.
They know—they exist together.
Soft fingers touching the
hard—soft—rough skin of rocks,
rocks of tenderness and beauty.
They know that feeling and they are a rock.
No doubt!
They let me touch them—climb them
and let me feel the warms of their bodies.
The night is calling—
calling to a new dance,
the dance of desert rocks.

SOUPS

S OUPS ARE GREAT. They can be a complete meal, a great side dish for a special dinner, a healthy snack when you are in a hurry, or a warming meal on cold days. I know in California it is almost never cold, but when I think about cold days, I am dreaming about Germany's cold rainy days when I had many hot, steaming soups to make me feel good. Do I miss that? No! But I am happy that I can dream about it. Back to soups.

HOW TO MAKE CREAMY SOUPS

1. Sauté ingredients in oil or ghee. You can use onions, garlic, ginger, celery, carrots, tomatoes. Add spices, herbs, a little water and sauté all until soft. Let it cool down a little and puree in blender, add tofu if desired and blend until smooth. Put back into pot, add water, stock or broth and heat up. Do not boil. Season more if needed.

2. Sauté as above, but add liquid after 5 minutes and simmer until vegetables are soft. Puree with electric hand blender. If the recipe asks for tofu, than scoop some soup into the blender, add tofu, puree until smooth and pour back into the soup. Stir well. Do not boil any more. This way the soup won't be as creamy and smooth.

HOW TO MAKE HEARTY SOUPS

If you are using different kinds of vegetables, be aware that they have different cooking times. Always start with the kind that needs the most time and add the rest later. For example, if you are using onions, carrots, broccoli, cauliflower and zucchini, you would first sauté the onions then add the carrots and the cauliflower, because they need a similar time to cook. Then you would add broccoli and when the soup is almost done, add the zucchini. Zucchini is a very soft vegetable and does not need to cook long.

There are three different kinds of recipes. Those with:

> exact measurements
> rough measurements
> no measurements

Just remember that it is easy to add spices to a soup or to any dish you are preparing, but it is difficult to take them out. So be gentle with seasonings and always taste before you put more in.

TOMATO BASIL SOUP

This soup is very easy to prepare, especially if you use canned tomatoes. If you are using fresh tomatoes remove the skins. The easiest way is to put the tomatoes in a bowl and pour boiling water over them. Let sit for 3-5 minutes. Now the skin peels off very easily.

> 1-2 tablespoons oil or ghee
> 1 medium size onion, diced
> 1 clove garlic, minced
> 3 celery stalks, sliced
> 1/2 can tomato paste
> 1 can chunky tomatoes or
> 6-8 fresh tomatoes
> 1/2 bunch fresh basil
> tamari or salt, dash
> black pepper, dash
> 1/2 cup water or soy milk
> 1/4 pound soft tofu, optional

Heat oil or ghee, add onions, garlic, celery and sauté for 5 minutes. Add tomato paste, tomatoes, water, basil, tamari or salt and simmer for about 15 minutes. Add black pepper if desired. Puree soup and tofu in blender. If you need more liquid add water or soy milk.

THAI RED LENTIL SOUP

1 1/2 cups red lentils
1 bunch lemon grass
1-2 tablespoons oil or ghee
medium size onion, diced
1-2 stalks celery
1-2 carrots, sliced
1-3 cloves garlic, minced
1/2 teaspoon fresh ginger, minced
tamari or salt
1/4 teaspoon cumin
yogurt, optional
1 can coconut milk

Wash lentils several times until water is clear. Cut lemon grass into pitcher and pour boiling water over it (3-4 cups) and let it sit for 10 minutes. Heat oil or ghee, add onion, garlic and ginger, sauté for 5 minutes. Add celery, carrots, lentils, lemon grass water and simmer for 20 minutes or until lentils are soft. Add salt or tamari, cumin and coconut milk. Do not boil. Add more lemon grass water if necessary. Take one scoop out into the blender, cream it and pour it back into the soup. Serve with yogurt on top.

GERMAN ERBSENSUPPE

This is a soup for cold days. When I was a child my mother used to make it on cold winter days and I loved it. It was made the real German way with bacon and sausage. This recipe is the real German way without the meat. Enjoy the taste.

    2 cups whole green dried peas, soaked overnight
    1-2 tablespoons oil
    medium size onion, diced
    2-4 carrots, sliced
    1-3 celery stalks, sliced
    4 cups water or vegetable broth
    6 soywiener sausage
    parsley, chopped
    tamari or salt
    black pepper

Heat oil and sauté onion for 5 minutes. Add carrots, celery, drained peas and vegetable broth or water and let it simmer for almost 1 hour or until peas are soft. Stir frequently, add more water if necessary. Season with salt or tamari and black pepper. Heat soy sausage in the soup whole or sliced. Serve with parsley on top.

CARROT CREAM SOUP

This is a very light and tasty soup.

    1-2 tablespoons oil or ghee
    onion, diced
    2-4 celery stalks, sliced
    5-10 carrots, sliced
    4-5 cups water or vegetable broth

tamari or salt
cayenne pepper, dash
curry, dash, optional
1/2 tablespoon dill, fresh or dried
1/4 pound soft tofu, optional

Sauté onion in oil or ghee, add celery and carrots and sauté for 5 minutes. Add water or vegetable broth, salt or tamari and all other spices. Simmer for 10 minutes or until vegetables are soft. Add more water if necessary. Use blender or hand mixer to puree soup. Turn heat down. Add pureed tofu. Variation: Add cilantro, parsley or sautéed spinach.

CARROT ZUCCHINI SOUP

oil
medium onion, diced
clove garlic, minced
celery stalks, sliced
carrots, sliced medium thick
4-5 cups water or vegetable broth
zucchini, sliced
1/2 bunch parsley, chopped
tamari or salt
black pepper or cayenne
curry, dash, optional

Heat oil and sauté onion, garlic, celery and carrots for 5 minutes. Add water or vegetable broth and salt or tamari. Simmer for 10 minutes. Add zucchini and parsley and simmer for another 5 minutes, or until zucchini is done. Add spices. Take one scoop out and blend, pour back into the soup. You can use cilantro instead of parsley to give the soup a different taste.

MIXED VEGETABLE SOUP A LA RON

A friend invited me for dinner and served this great vegetable soup, which I really liked. I am happy to share his recipe with you. It looks like a lot of work, but it will not take you more then 1/2 hour to prepare.

1 tablespoon oil
onion, diced
celery stalks, sliced
1/4 cup brown rice, washed
1 can navy beans, 15 oz. or
1 cup dried beans soaked over night
1/4 cup red lentils, washed
2 potatoes, diced
2 carrots, diced
1 leek stalk, sliced
5 mushrooms, sliced
2 stems broccoli, cut in small roses, stalk optional
4-5 cups water
1 cube vegetable broth
marjoram, oregano
tamari or salt
black pepper, optional

Sauté onion and celery in oil until soft, puree in blender and set aside. Heat rice in pot, stir for 1 minute. Add water, vegetable broth, navy beans, onion-celery puree, lentils and all vegetables, except broccoli, and all spices. Simmer for 35 minutes, add broccoli and simmer for 10 minutes more.

PUMPKIN YAM SOUP

When you have had enough pumpkin pie then try this delicious pumpkin soup.

2 tablespoons ghee
1 teaspoon fresh ginger, minced
garlic, minced
onion, diced
3 cups pumpkin, coarsely diced
3 cups yams, coarsely diced
4 cups water or vegetable broth
dash: cumin, nutmeg, cayenne pepper
1 tablespoon tamari
1/4 bunch tarragon, optional

Sauté ginger, garlic, onion in ghee. Add pumpkin, yams, spices and water. Simmer for 35 minutes. Use electric hand blender to puree soup. Add tarragon and let sit for 5 minutes.

POTATO LEEK SOUP

This soup is light and you can eat it warm or cold.

2 tablespoons ghee
1 onion, diced
2 leek stalks, sliced
4-5 potatoes, diced
4 cups water
1 tablespoon vegetable broth
1/2 bunch tarragon, minced
dash: nutmeg, thyme, black pepper
tamari or salt

Sauté onion and leeks in ghee for 5 minutes. Add potatoes, water, broth, tarragon and tamari or salt. Simmer for 15 minutes or until soft. Take one scoop out and mix in blender, and put it back into the pot. Add spices. Use electric hand blender to puree the soup. Serve warm or cold.

GARDEN POTPOURRI

    1-2 tablespoons oil
    onion, quartered
    garlic, minced
    2-3 carrots, sliced
    2-3 leek stalks, sliced
    4-5 potatoes, diced
    4 cups water & 1 tablespoon vegetable broth
    1/4 bunch tarragon
    dash: nutmeg, thyme, black pepper
    tamari or salt

Heat oil. Sauté onion and garlic for 2 minutes. Add carrots, leeks, potatoes, tarragon, tamari or salt, water and vegetable broth. Simmer for 5 minutes, add spices and simmer for 5 minutes more, or until done.

MISO VEGETABLE SOUP

    oil
    1 onion, quartered
    2 carrots, sliced
    2 zucchini, sliced
    cauliflower, small roses
    snow peas
    4 tablespoons miso

5 cups hot water
1/2 pound firm tofu, diced, optional
tamari.

Heat oil. Sauté all vegetables for 2 minutes. Add hot water and bring to a boil. Turn heat down. Mix miso with 1 cup soup and pour back into the pot. Do not boil the soup after adding miso! Add tofu if desired. Soup is ready when vegetables are soft. Add more tamari and/or miso if necessary.

LENTIL SOUP

1-2 tablespoons oil
onion quartered
garlic
carrots
1-2 potatoes, optional
2 cups lentils, washed
2-4 cups water or vegetable broth
cumin, dash
black pepper, dash
salt or tamari
1/2 teaspoon vinegar, optional
1 piece kombu, optional
cilantro, optional

Sauté onion, garlic, carrots and potatoes in oil for about 5 minutes. Then add lentils and water or broth. Add kombu now and take it out after 10-15 minutes. Heat to a boil, then simmer until lentils are soft. Stir once in a while and add more water if necessary. Add salt or tamari, cumin and cilantro. Add vinegar.

CHILI CON TOFU

This soup is great. It is a whole meal, especially when served with cornbread and salad. Freeze the tofu at least for 3 days.

1-2 tablespoons oil
1-2 onions
1-2 cloves garlic
3-5 carrots
celery
2-4 green bell peppers
1/2 can tomato puree
1 can crushed tomatoes, or
4 fresh tomatoes
frozen or canned corn
1 cup red chili or kidney beans, soaked over night and then cooked
or canned beans
1/2 pound firm frozen tofu, defrosted
salt
2-4 teaspoons chili powder
cayenne pepper, dash

Squeeze out tofu and break up in small pieces. Season with salt and chili powder. Sauté onions and garlic for about 5 minutes, then add tofu and stir well. Add all vegetables and sauté for 5 minutes. Add chili powder, tomato puree and canned or fresh tomatoes. (Take off skin. To do that, pour boiling water over tomatoes and let them sit for 10 minutes. Now it is very easy to take off the skin). Cut into chunks.

Add beans, 2 cups water and stir. Let the soup simmer for 3 minutes. Add more water if desired, and stir once in a while. Add corn, salt and spices and simmer for 10 minutes more. Serve over fresh baked cornbread.

SPINACH SOUP

If you feel like eating something green, then this is the perfect meal for you.

  1 teaspoon oil
  3-4 bunches spinach
  1 onion, diced
  1 clove garlic
  3-4 cups water
  1/4 pound soft tofu
  salt
  pepper
  nutmeg

Sauté onion and garlic in oil. Add washed spinach and sauté for 5 minutes more. Add water and let simmer for 5-7 minutes. Spice with salt, black pepper and nutmeg. Puree soup and tofu in blender. Pour back into the pot.

ONE ROSE AFFAIR

The rose given
with an open heart
showed her beauty, her softness.
Let me smell you, taste you, touch you,
knowing there are no roses
without a thorn.
A moment of bliss,
total presence,
melting into each other.
The rose is gone,
went back from where she came.
What stayed is the beauty,
the beauty of the affair.

Fire Dance, 1987
Pastel on paper

SALADS

SALADS OFFER A WORLD of possibilities. They can be a meal in themselves. They also can be used as colorful art on your table. Spices and color combination are very important. If you are going to prepare a salad, take a moment, close your eyes and visualize the color combination you want. Just imagine you want to use spinach in combination with something else. I personally would go for taste and a color suitable with green, such as orange, red, white, yellow, and the taste could be sweet or sweet and sour, or spicy. I might choose:

for orange: yams, carrots, oranges...
for red: tomatoes, red bell peppers, red radish...
for yellow: corn, yellow squash, melon...
for white: cauliflower, mung beans, mushrooms...

I also can choose a combination of colors or keep it all green. Now I decide what flavors I want to give my salad and which vegetables I would like to combine with spinach. After I have chosen the vegetables or fruit (the two together only if you do not worry about food combining, since fruit and vegetables do not actually digest well together) I decide which dressing I want. Be creative and take a risk, that is the best way to learn. All recipes can be changed easily so that they have your own signature. A recipe should be seen only as an idea. Take from recipes only what you need and ignore the rest. Allow yourself to create some meals that taste different than you thought they would. That is how you find out what to change the next time.

CURRY RICE SALAD

If you like a spicy taste, try this salad.

> 2-3 cups cooked brown rice
> 1 celery stalk, diced
> 2 green onions, thinly sliced
> 1 red bell pepper, diced
> 1 carrot, diced
> 5 mushrooms, sautéed, optional
> 1/2 can corn

DRESSING

> 1/2 pound soft tofu
> 1 tablespoon tamari
> 1 tablespoon curry
> juice of 1/2 orange
> cumin, dash
> water if desired

Mix in bowl: rice and all vegetables. Puree tofu, tamari, curry, orange juice and cumin in blender, pour over rice mixture and stir.

STEAMED VEGETABLE SALAD

> 1/4 head cauliflower roses
> 1-2 bunch broccoli roses
> 2-4 carrots, sliced
> snow peas, some
> 1-3 zucchini

Steam all vegetables separately because they all have a different steaming time. Hint: If you want to keep the vegetables bright in color, dip them briefly into ice water immediately after steaming and drain.

1/4 cup olive oil or less
2 tablespoons vinegar
1 tablespoon lemon juice
1 clove garlic, pressed
1 teaspoon mustard
2 teaspoons tamari
cayenne pepper, dash
1 tablespoon water

Mix and pour over salad and let sit for 15 minutes.

SPINACH YAM SALAD

If you have had a lot of mixed green salads and you want to try somthing different, this is the one.

2-3 bunches spinach, washed and stemmed
2-3 yams peeled, diced and steamed,
leave 1/2 steamed yam for dressing.

DRESSING
(see Orange Yam Dressing under "Salad Dressings")

GREEN BEAN MUSHROOM SALAD

This is a great salad. It takes a little more time to prepare. It is worth it.

    1 pound string beans
    1 pound mushrooms, same size
    2 onions, quartered
    2 red bell peppers, diced to medium size pieces
    4-5 cloves garlic, whole
    2 tablespoons olive oil
    1/4 teaspoon salt
    1/4 teaspoon crushed red pepper flakes
    dash: black pepper, oregano

Turn baking oven to 375°F. Steam beans 5 minutes or until soft but still crunchy, and let cool down or, better, dip in ice water. Mix together in a baking dish all other ingredients and bake for 15-20 minutes or until mushrooms are soft. Let cool before pouring over green beans.

SPICY GARBANZO A LA MOROCCO

If you like it hot and spicy try this one. It goes great with humus.

    1-2 cups garbanzo beans, soaked overnight then cooked in fresh
       water until soft but not mushy
    2 teaspoons olive oil
    3 cloves garlic, minced
    1/4 teaspoon curry
    1/4 teaspoon cumin
    1/4 teaspoon red pepper flakes
    salt, dash
    1/4 cup water

Heat oil, add garlic and all spices, add cooked garbanzo beans, salt and water, and bring to a boil. Reduce heat and simmer for about 15 minutes. Eat warm or cold in pita bread.

HUMUS

1-2 cups garbanzo beans, soaked overnight and then cooked in
    fresh water
1-2 tablespoons tahini
1-2 cloves garlic
3-4 tablespoons olive oil
2-3 tablespoons lemon juice
3 tablespoons water
salt
black pepper
cumin, dash

Use food processor to mix all ingredients together. If it is too thick add more water.

GERMAN BEET SALAD

You can use red or golden beets. Both are good for this salad. Golden beets are sweeter in taste but not as easy to find. Leaves and stems are great to steam or sauté and eat separately.

4-6 whole beets, cooked, peeled, and diced
1 teaspoon lemon juice
1 teaspoon honey
1/2 teaspoon apple cider vinegar
salt, dash

3-4 drops sesame oil, optional
1/2 teaspoon fresh dill

Mix all ingredients together and serve at room temperature.

BEET APPLE SALAD

2-3 beets
1-2 apples
2-3 tablespoons lemon juice
1 teaspoon honey

Grate raw beets medium fine. Grate apples. Mix all ingredients together.
Serve with rice nut loaf.

SZECHWAN SOBA NOODLES

This is a great salad, if you do not want to use wheat pasta. Soba noodles are made out of buckwheat. You can buy them at health food stores or Japanese, Thai or Chinese markets.

1-1 1/2 packages Soba noodles, cooked
2-3 carrots, diced small
10-15 snow peas, steamed
1 red bell pepper
1-2 zucchini, diced small

Possible substitutes: broccoli, steamed mushrooms, sautéed mung beans.

DRESSING

1/4 teaspoon hot sesame oil
1-2 tablespoons tahini
tofu, soft
tamari
1-2 tablespoons lemon juice
garlic, minced
fresh ginger, minced
1-2 tablespoons nutritional yeast
cayenne pepper

Mix all ingredients in blender and pour over cooked, cold noodles and vegetables.

SPICY BLACK BEAN SALAD

This is an easy salad after a Mexican meal, when you have black beans left over.

3-4 cups cooked black beans
1 red bell pepper, diced
1/2 can corn
1/2 bunch cilantro
crushed red pepper flakes, dash
cumin, dash
juice of 1/2 lemon
salt

Mix everything together and serve at room temperature.

WILD RICE SALAD

1¼ cups wild rice, cooked
1 jar capers
1-2 stalks celery, diced
½ bunch parsley, minced
1-2 zucchini, diced
1-2 carrots, diced
1 red bell pepper, optional

Sauté the carrots, bell pepper, celery and zucchini for about 4-5 minutes and add this as well as the parsley and the capers to the rice. Prepare the dressing and pour over the salad. Let sit for 15 minutes before serving.

DRESSING

2-4 tablespoons balsamic vinegar
1-3 tablespoons olive oil
1 teaspoon tamari
salt, cayenne, black pepper

Mix all ingredients in blender and pour over salad.

SEAWEED SALAD

I know that not everybody likes seaweed. I never cooked with it, because I did not like it. But one day I wanted to explore something new and so I created this salad. Most people who have tasted it like it a lot.

½ package wakame
½ package hijiki
1 red bell pepper, diced

1 tablespoon sesame oil
tamari
balsamic vinegar
sesame seeds, toasted

Put wakame and hijiki in separate bowls and cover with hot water. Soak for about 15 minutes, then rinse under fresh water and drain. Heat sesame oil in frying pan, add hijiki and fry for about 6 minutes or until a little crisp. Add the bell pepper, fry for a moment and then add wakame and tamari. Stir well. Before you add the wakame, cut out the hard middle part. Let it cool. Add a little balsamic vinegar and serve with sesame seeds on top.

LENTIL TABULI SALAD

1 cup lentils
3 cups water
salt
cumin, dash
1 cup tabuli mix
1½ cups hot water
1-2 tomatoes, diced
1 bunch parsley, minced
1-2 teaspoons balsamic vinegar
1-2 teaspoons olive oil
salt, to taste
cayenne pepper

Cook washed lentils in 3 cups water until they are soft, but not mushy. Add more water if necessary. Season with salt and cumin. Cool in refrigerator for about 15 minutes. Mix tabuli with hot water, cover and refrigerate for about 30 minutes. Combine parsley, tomatoes, lentils and tabuli. Season with vinegar, olive oil, salt and cayenne pepper. Serve with pita bread and humus.

RAITA

Raita is a great side dish for a spicy Indian dinner because it is cooling.

2-3 cucumbers
3-4 tablespoons yogurt
cumin, dash
salt, dash

Peel cucumbers with a potato peeler. Slice them lengthwise in half and take out the seeds with a teaspoon. Dice cucumbers in medium size pieces. In a bowl mix yogurt, cumin and salt. Use a whisk to make it smooth. Add cucumbers and stir.

LET IT FLOW

Love comes in.
Love is joy.
Sees the pain,
takes it away
Eyes are so full,
full of
ocean and mountain.
Let me fly and be inside,
inside the water
of blue sky.
Skin of my face
feels like a flower,
a flower in the dawn.
I am free,
free like a bird in the sky.

SALAD DRESSINGS

DRESSINGS ARE VERY IMPORTANT for the taste of the salad you are preparing. You don't want to overpower the unique flavors of the vegetables or greens you are using. I like to make my dressings in a blender. That makes them creamy. There are many options what to put into your dressing. The basic recipe has:

> olive oil,
> vinegar,
> lemon juice,
> mustard,
> water,
> salt or tamari.

From there you can add and create what you want. Be adventurous and you will find your favorite dressing. I have tried capers, parsley, spinach, lettuce, watermelon and tahini. If you are using tahini or avocado you need less or no olive oil.

DILL DRESSING
makes 1 cup

1/2 cup olive oil
2 tablespoons raspberry vinegar
2 tablespoons lemon juice
1 teaspoon mustard
1 teaspoon honey
2 teaspoons nutritional yeast
1 clove garlic, minced
1/2 bunch dill or
1 tablespoon dried dill
1/2 teaspoon salt
1/4 cup & 1 tablespoon water

Combine all ingredients in a blender and mix briefly.

ORANGE YAM DRESSING
makes 1 cup

1/2 cup fresh orange juice
2 tablespoons olive oil
1 tablespoon balsamic vinegar
1 teaspoon lemon juice
1 clove garlic, minced
1-2 teaspoons tamari
cayenne pepper
1/2 yam, steamed

Peel yam and cut into medium size pieces. Steam for 5 minutes or until soft. Let cool down. Combine all ingredients in a blender and mix. This dressing is great on spinach.

AVOCADO CILANTRO DRESSING
makes 1 cup

1/4 cup olive oil
1/2 avocado or less
2 tablespoons lemon juice
1-2 teaspoons mustard
2 teaspoon nutritional yeast
1 teaspoon honey
1 clove garlic, minced
2 tablespoons apple cider vinegar
1/2 bunch cilantro (parsley, lettuce or spinach may be substituted)
1/4 cup water
1/4 teaspoon salt

Combine all ingredients in a blender and mix.

TAHINI CARROT DRESSING
makes 2 1/2 cups

1/2 cup tahini
1 cup fresh carrot juice
1/2 cup water
2 tablespoons lemon juice
1 1/2 teaspoons balsamic vinegar
2 tablespoons tamari
2 teaspoons nutritional yeast
1/2 teaspoon honey
1 teaspoon garlic, minced
cayenne pepper, dash

Combine all ingredients in a blender and mix.

VINAIGRETTE

1/2 cup olive oil
2 tablespoons apple cider vinegar
1 teaspoon honey
1 teaspoon Dijon mustard
1 teaspoon dill
salt
black pepper

Combine all ingredients in a bowl and mix with a whisk. This is a great dressing for potato salad.

TOFU CURRY DRESSING
(see Curry Rice Salad under "Salads")

SAUCES

INDONESIAN PEANUT SAUCE
(see Gado Gado under "Entrées")

TOFU CILANTRO CREAM SAUCE

This is a great sauce for vegetables. Sauté the vegetables and when they are almost done, pour cilantro cream over them and heat up slowly. Do not boil.

    1 pound soft tofu
    garlic, minced
    1-2 bunches cilantro, minced
    tamari
    cayenne pepper, dash
    1/4-1/2 cup soy milk

Mix all ingredients in blender. Start with 1/4 cup soy milk and add more if desired. Instead of cilantro you also can use parsley.

MUSHROOM GRAVY

    2-3 cups mushrooms
    2 tablespoons butter
    1 onion, minced
    1 clove garlic
    1/2 cup soy milk
    1 tablespoon whole wheat flour

salt
black pepper

Clean mushrooms and then separate stems and caps. Use food processor to mash up the stems. Sauté onion and garlic in butter until soft. Add mushroom mousse and sauté for 5 minutes more. Sprinkle flour into it and stir well. Slowly add the soy milk, stirring all the time. Let it boil once, then turn heat down. Add more soy milk if sauce is too thick. Season with salt and pepper. Slice mushroom caps, sauté in little oil and add to the gravy. This sauce is great with mashed potatoes and Rice Nut Loaf.

SALSA

It is not a Mexican meal without salsa. Picante, muy picante.

> 4-6 tomatoes, diced
> 1 onion, minced
> 1/4 bunch cilantro, minced
> 1-3 green hot chili peppers, minced
> 1-2 tablespoons lemon juice
> salt

Mix all ingredients together and let sit for 15 minutes at room temperature before serving.

GUACAMOLE

> 2-3 avocados
> 2 tomatoes, diced
> 1/4 bunch cilantro, minced
> 1-2 tablespoons lemon juice

1-2 cloves garlic, minced
1/2 teaspoon cumin
salt
1/2-1 jalepeño pepper

Mash avocados and drizzle lemon juice over them so that the avocados do not turn brown. Add all other ingredients and mix well.

TOFU SOUR CREAM

Whenever you would use sour cream, this is a great substitute.

1 pound soft tofu
1 tablespoon oil
1 tablespoon nutritional yeast
2 tablespoons lemon juice
2 tablespoons rice vinegar
salt

Mix tofu in a blender or food processor until smooth, then add all other ingredients and blend for a moment more.

TOFU RICOTTA

1 pound firm tofu
1/4 cup olive oil
1/2 teaspoon nutmeg
salt

Mix all ingredients in a blender or food processor. If you like the ricotta firmer, add more tofu to the mixture, but do not use the blender any more.

TOFU FETA

1 pound firm tofu
1 tablespoon oil
1 tablespoon apple cider vinegar
2 tablespoons lemon juice
2 tablespoons nutritional yeast
1 tablespoon dill
2 tablespoons green onion, sliced
salt

Mix all ingredients in a blender or food processor.

ALMOND MAYONNAISE

1/2 cup raw almonds, blanched
1/2 cup soy milk
1/2 clove garlic, minced or
1/4 teaspoon garlic powder
1 teaspoon nutritional yeast
salt
1 cup oil
2-3 tablespoons lemon juice
1/2-1 teaspoon apple cider vinegar

To blanch almonds, cover them with boiling water and when cool enough, slip off the skin. Use blender or food processor to grind them. Add the soy milk and blend to a fine paste. Mix in garlic, yeast and salt. With motor running, slowly add the oil. If the mayonnaise is not thick enough, add a little more oil. Keep motor running when you add lemon juice and vinegar. Refrigerate at least 1/2 hour before serving. That helps to thicken the mayonnaise.

TARRAGON SAUCE
(see Tarragon Vegetable Casserole under "Entrées")

ALMOND SAUCE

1/2 cup blanched almonds
1/2-3/4 cup water
salt
cayenne pepper
2 tablespoons lemon juice, optional

Grind almonds in blender to fine paste. Slowly add water and all other ingredients. Add more water if you like the sauce thinner.

SWEET SAUCES
(see Vanilla Sauce & Carob/Chocolate Sauce under "Desserts")

❧

MOUNTAIN WIND

Life wind is blowing on this beautiful mountain.
It's coming to greet you,
To play with you
to love you,
to feel the coolness on your skin.
Life is like this wind,
embracing you with a warm breeze.

Landscape, 1993
Tempera on paper

CHUTNEYS

PEAR ORANGE CHUTNEY

4-5 cups pears, chopped
1 tablespoon garlic, chopped
2 cups honey
1 1/2 cups raisins
1/2 cup fresh ginger, minced
1 1/2 teaspoons salt
1/4 teaspoon cayenne
1 1/2 cups apple cider vinegar
1/2 cup orange juice

Place all ingredients in a pot and simmer until the fruit is soft. Add more spices if desired.

APPLE LEMON CHUTNEY
(makes about 1 1/2 quarts)

1 organic lemon, chopped
1 tablespoon garlic, chopped
5 cups apples, chopped
2 cups honey
1 1/2 cups raisins
1/2 cup fresh ginger, minced
1 1/2 teaspoons salt

65

1/4 teaspoon cayenne
1/4 teaspoon red pepper flakes
2 cups apple cider vinegar

Place all ingredients in a pot and simmer until the fruit is soft.

PINEAPPLE CHUTNEY

1 ripe pineapple
2-3 tablespoons ghee
1 onion, diced
1 1/2 teaspoons cumin seeds
1 1/2 teaspoons coriander seeds
1-2 teaspoons crushed pepper flakes
1/2 teaspoon cardamom seeds
1/4 cup honey or maple syrup
1/2 cup raisins

Peel, quarter, core and cut pineapple into small pieces. Sauté onion in ghee for about 5 minutes. Add red pepper flakes, cumin and corriander seeds and fry until dark but not burned. Add the pineapple, cardamom seeds and allspice. Simmer until fruit is tender. Keep stirring, so it won't burn. Add sweetener and raisins and cook on low heat until the chutney is thick.

TOFUS

I HEAR A LOT OF PEOPLE saying that they don't like tofu, or that tofu really has no taste and that anyway they just don't know how to prepare it. Here are some recipes that indicate how to use tofu in different and tasty ways.

SCRAMBLED TOFU

1 pound firm tofu
1 tablespoon tamari
1 teaspoon curry
handful mushrooms, sliced
1-2 zucchini, diced
1 red bell pepper, diced
1/2 bunch green onion, thin sliced
1/2 onion, diced
salt
black pepper

Take tofu out of the water and mush it into a bowl. Add tamari and curry. Mix well and set aside. Sauté onions and green onions in oil, add red bell pepper and after 2 minutes add mushrooms and then zucchini. Season with salt and pepper. Add tofu and stir well. Sauté for 5 minutes more. Add more spices if desired.

MARINATED BAKED TOFU SLICES

1 pound firm tofu
1/4 cup tamari
1/4 cup water
1 teaspoon garlic, minced
1 tablespoon mustard
1 tablespoon nutritional yeast
1 teaspoon honey
cayenne pepper
sesame seeds, optional

Cut tofu into 8 slices and put into a baking pan. Combine all ingredients for the marinade in a small bowl and mix with a whisk. Pour the marinade over tofu. Heat baking oven to 400°F and bake for about 20 minutes or until liquid is dissolved and tofu is brown and crispy.

TOFU PATTIES

1/2 cup cooked rice
1 carrot, diced
1 onion, minced
2 green onions, sliced thin
1/2 cup almonds, chopped fine
1 pound firm tofu
2-3 tablespoons either oat, quinoa or rice flour
1/2 cup water with 1 teaspoon arrowroot
tamari or salt
cayenne pepper
1/2 teaspoon oregano
1 cup quinoa flour

Sauté all vegetables. Mix in a bowl all ingredients except the 1 cup quinoa flour. Add the sauteed vegetables. Mix well and, with wet hands, form small patties. Dip each side in quinoa flour and fry in a little oil until brown and crispy.

BREAKFAST POTATOES

POTATOES AU GRATIN

4-6 red rose potatoes
1 cup tofu sour cream
1 cup soy cheese, grated
Mix together:
    2 teaspoons marjoram
    1/2 teaspoon salt
    1/2 teaspoon black pepper

Slice potatoes very thin. Oil baking pan and put one layer potatoes into bottom. Sprinkle with marjoram mixture and cover with a thin layer of tofu sour cream. Repeat the layer, but use soy cheese instead of sour cream. Make four to six layers. Finish with a layer of potatoes. Cover with parchment paper and aluminum foil. Bake at 400°F for almost 2 hours. Take off foil, sprinkle with soy cheese and bake for 10 minutes more.

ROSEMARY POTATOES

4-6 potatoes
1 teaspoon rosemary
2 tablespoons olive oil
salt
pepper

Cut potatoes in medium size pieces. Pour olive oil over potatoes, season with salt, pepper and rosemary. Let sit for 15 minutes. Heat oven to 375°F. Put potatoes on a baking sheet and bake for 30 to 40 minutes. Stir once in a while. Serve with scrambled tofu and a salad.

POTATO DELIGHT

4 raw potatoes
1 onion
handful mushrooms
2 carrots, grated
2 zucchini, sliced
1 red bell pepper
dill
1 1/2 cup tofu sour cream
1/2 cup water with 1 teaspoon arrowroot
1 tablespoon oat bran or wheat germ
salt
black pepper

Grate potatoes and set aside. Sauté onion and mushrooms, add zucchini and bell pepper. Spice with salt and pepper. Combine potatoes, carrots, dill and sautéed vegetables in large bowl. Mix in arrowroot, tofu sour cream and oat bran. Spread into well greased pan. Cover with aluminum foil and bake for 1 1/2 hours. Take off foil and bake for 15 minutes more.

LOVE

When I was little
I felt love in my body
and in my heart.
Love was so light, so colorful,
without fear.
My heart was open
and full of joy.
Then I grew older
and love wasn't love anymore.
I didn't know what it was.
I learned to hide it, to close my heart.
Suddenly, love was fear, was sex
was heavy and judged.
Love without heart,
also no love.
I always knew, that I was missing something
in my life.
My body knew
my heart knew.
A life without love
is no life,
is no joy.
It took me many years
to allow myself to feel again,
to feel my body and my heart.
Now I know

it is a part of me.
No one can take it away.
I accept this part in me
My love—my heart.
I'm happy that I can love myself
and experience love again.

Mystic Path, 1993
Acrylic on paper

ENTRÉES

WHEN I THINK OF ENTRÉES, I imagine traveling; there is such a wonderful variety of tastes to experience in places such as Italy, Germany, Mexico, Thailand, the exotic Bali, or whatever country to which you choose to "travel." In the following recipes you will find a number of ways to explore meatless entrees which are tasty, satisfying and healthy. For those of you who enjoy cooking and planning festive meals, the entrée as "middle" course can serve as a link between your soup/salad and dessert, setting the tone for the entire meal. A nourishing entrée is the key to a complete and fulfilling dining experience!

STIR-FRY VEGETABLES WITH BAKED TOFU

This is a light and delicious meal, which is easy and quick to prepare. Start with the tofu, because it needs to sit in the marinade for a while.

BAKED MARINATED TOFU

1 pound tofu, firm
1/2 cup tamari
1/2 cup water
2 tablespoons lemon juice
1 clove garlic, pressed
1 tablespoon fresh ginger, grated
1 teaspoon mustard

1/4 teaspoon cumin
cayenne pepper, dash
teaspoon curry, optional
1/2 tablespoon nutritional yeast, optional

Cut tofu into 8 slices. Layer tofu into a baking pan. Stir remaining ingredients together and pour over tofu. Turn oven to 400°F. Bake tofu for 20 minutes or until liquid is dissolved and tofu is light brown and crispy. Serve hot with the stir fry. The stir fry should have a variety of vegetables. Use the ones you like best the most.

STIR-FRY

1-2 onions
1-2 cloves garlic
1 tablespoon fresh ginger, grated
2-4 carrots, cut into sticks
1/4 head of cauliflower, roses
1-2 stems broccoli, roses
mushrooms, a few
2-3 zucchini
mung beans
snow peas
1 tablespoon tamari
cumin, optional

Prepare in a wok if you have one, otherwise use a pot. Heat some oil and start with onions, garlic and ginger. Sauté for 5 minutes then add carrots and cauliflower. Cover and after 3-4 minutes add mushrooms and spices. Stir well, then add broccoli. Add zucchini and mung beans when the vegetables are almost done. Do not overcook! Serve with brown rice or quinoa and baked tofu or tofu patties.

MIDDLE EASTERN STUFFED ZUCCHINI

When I was still living in Germany, an Arabian family invited me to dinner. They served this wonderful stuffed zucchini dish. At that time I still was eating meat, so it was no problem that they included ground lamb along with feta cheese and raisins. Later I changed the recipe to vegetarian. The meat may be gone, but the Middle Eastern flavor is still there, and I think it tastes great this way.

4 zucchini
3 tablespoons oil
1 onion
2 cloves garlic
3/4 cup water with 1 teaspoon arrowroot
1/2 cup tofu feta
3/4 cup soy cheese
fresh parsley
fresh dill
3/4 cup bulghur
2 tablespoons flour
salt, dash
pepper, dash
paprika powder

Slice zucchini lengthwise. Scoop out the inside and chop fine. Sauté with onion and garlic. Save the shells until later. Pour 3/4 cup boiling water over bulghur and let sit for 1/2 hour. Combine flour, cheese, herbs, arrowroot, bulghur, spices and tofu feta with sautéed zucchini pulp. Mix well. Fill the zucchini shells. Pour 3/4 cup water into a baking dish. Place stuffed zucchini into it, cover with aluminum foil and bake at 375°F for 20-30 minutes. Sprinkle with paprika powder and serve with brown rice or baguette bread and a big salad.

LASAGNA
(8 servings)

Lasagna is great for a party, because you can prepare it a day ahead and bake it when you need it. Try the lasagna made with carrot-beet sauce instead of tomato sauce. It is something different and more healthy. Prepare the carrot-beet sauce first, because it needs to cook awhile.

CARROT-BEET SAUCE

1 onion, diced
2 cloves garlic, minced
6-8 carrots, sliced thick
1-2 beets, diced
2-3 cups water
1 teaspoon oregano
salt or tamari
pepper

Sauté onion and garlic for about 5 minutes. Add carrots and beets and sauté for 5 more minutes. Add 2 cups water, salt or tamari, pepper and oregano. Simmer until carrots and beets are soft. Turn heat off and puree with an electric hand blender. Add more water if necessary.

LASAGNA

2 tablespoons oil
2 cloves garlic
1 onion
3-4 bunches spinach, chopped
1 red bell pepper, diced
2 pounds tofu ricotta
1 pound soy cheese, grated

salt
pepper
3/4 cup spinach water with 1 teaspoon arrowroot
1 bunch parsley, chopped
1 can corn, optional
1/2 pound soy mozzarella cheese
lasagna noodles
carrot-beet sauce (see recipe on previous page)

Sauté onion and garlic for 5 minutes. Add washed spinach, salt and pepper and sauté until spinach is soft. Drain spinach and keep the spinach water and dissolve the arrowroot in it. Combine tofu ricotta, soy cheese, parsley, corn and spinach in a bowl, and mix well. Roast bell pepper in a frying pan without using oil and add to spinach mixture. Grate the tofu mozzarella. Cook the pasta. Now you are ready to layer the lasagna. Oil a long baking dish; scoop some carrot-beet sauce into the bottom and put one layer of lasanga noodles on top of it, followed by a layer of spinach mixture; sprinkle with mozzarella and cover it with sauce. Repeat these layers, finishing with lasagna noodles and sauce on top. Cover with aluminum foil. Oil the aluminum foil, or use a piece of parchment paper between food and foil so that the aluminum doesn't touch the lasagna. Bake at 375°F for about 40 minutes, take off the foil, sprinkle tofu mozzarella on top and bake for 10 minutes more. Let cool for 15 minutes before cutting. Serve with homemade Italian bread and a big salad.

POLENTA SPINACH PIE

2 cups polenta
4-6 cups water
1 clove garlic
salt, pepper
cumin, dash
crushed red pepper flakes, dash
oregano
1-2 red bell peppers, diced
1 onion
2-3 pounds spinach
1 cup tofu cream
3/4 cup spinach water with 1 teaspoon arrowroot

The best way to cook polenta is in a double boiler. If you don't have one, use a big enough pot so you can stir easily. Bring water to a boil, turn heat down to low, then add the polenta and stir right away. Add salt and spices, stir, cover with a lid. Keep on low heat for about 30 minutes or until done. Add more water if it's too thick. It should have a creamy consistency.

For the filling: sauté onion, garlic and spinach. Set aside. Drain the spinach and save the water. Roast bell peppers in frying pan without using oil. Set aside. Mix tofu cream and arrowroot water with spinach. If more spices are needed add them now. Oil a baking dish and spread half of the polenta in a thin layer using a wet rubber spatula or by hand. Spread in the spinach mix. Add an even layer of red bell peppers and spread the rest of the polenta on top. Cover with aluminum foil and bake at 375°F for about 20 minutes. Take off the foil and bake for 15 minutes more. Let cool for 15 minutes before cutting. You also can serve tomato sauce over it. Variation: Instead of spinach use zucchini, carrots and corn.

TARRAGON VEGETABLE CASSEROLE

4-5 carrots, cut in big pieces
1/2 head of cauliflower, big roses
2 leeks, sliced
2 onions, quartered
2-3 zucchini
1 stem broccoli
salt, pepper
oregano, tarragon

Put all vegetables in a bowl, spice to taste and toss well. Layer onto an oiled baking dish.

Tarragon sauce:

3 tablespoons ghee, butter or oil
4 cloves garlic, diced
2 tablespoons whole wheat flour
2/3 cup water
1 bunch fresh tarragon
cayenne pepper
1 cup soy milk
1 tablespoon tahini
salt
cayenne pepper

Sauté garlic in heated ghee, butter or oil. Add flour and stir well. Slowly pour water into mixture, stirring all the time to eliminate lumps. Add tahini, soy milk and spices. If the sauce is too thick, add some more soy milk. Pour over the vegetables. Cover with aluminum foil and bake at 375°F for 40-50 minutes. Serve with brown rice and baked tofu or polenta steaks.

LENTIL-POTATO CASSEROLE

2 cups lentils, washed
4 cups water
1 onion
2 cloves garlic
1/2 bunch cilantro
salt, pepper
1 teaspoon oil
3-4 leeks
salt, pepper
4 potatoes, sliced
cheese, optional

Sauté onion and garlic. Add lentils and water and bring to a boil. Turn heat to low and let simmer until lentils are done. Add salt, pepper and cilantro. Quarter leeks lengthwise and cut into 3 inch sticks. Sauté in oil, add salt and pepper. Set aside. Slice raw potatoes. Oil baking dish and layer lentils on the bottom, then leeks and the potatoes on top. Cover with aluminum foil and bake at 375°F for about 45 minutes. Take off the foil and bake 10 minutes more or until potatoes are light brown. If you want to use cheese on top, do it now.

PASTA WITH GREEN VEGGIES

1 pound green beans
1-2 stems of broccoli
1 pound asparagus
2 zucchini
1-2 onions
1-2 cloves garlic

SAUCE

1 pound soft tofu
1 cup soy milk
1 tablespoon soy sauce
2 tablespoons nutritional yeast or
parmesan
cayenne, dash
cumin, dash optional
2 cloves garlic
5-6 leaves fresh basil

PASTA: WHOLE WHEAT OR SOBA NOODLES

Wash and cut all vegetables, keeping green beans whole. Steam green beans and asparagus separately. Sauté onion and garlic, add broccoli and cover pot for 5 minutes, add beans, asparagus and zucchini. Stir for a moment and then add sauce. For the cream sauce put all ingredients into a blender and mix. Use more seasoning if desired. Pour over vegetables. Heat but do not boil. In the meantime bring water for pasta to a boil, adding some drops of oil to prevent pasta from sticking. Serve with Italian salad and fresh baked bread.

PESTO

Pesto can be made in advance and kept in the refrigerator for about 3 days.

1/2 cup olive oil
1 cup pine nuts and/or cashews
3-5 cloves garlic
1-2 bunches fresh basil
2-4 tablespoons nutritional yeast

salt
black pepper
water (optional)

Use food processor or blender. Blend nuts, add oil and all other ingredients. Add a little water if desired. Serve with linguini or soba noodles, a fresh garden salad and homemade bread.

PASTA DE POMODORE

4-6 tomatoes, diced
1 onion, diced
2 cloves garlic, minced
1 pound mushrooms, sliced
2 roasted red bell peppers, medium diced
3/4 cup capers
3/4 cup black olives, sliced
5-6 sun dried tomatoes, diced
salt
cayenne pepper
3/4 teaspoon oregano

Sauté onion and garlic in a little oil. Add mushrooms and sauté for 5 minutes more. Add roasted bell pepper, olives and capers. Season with salt, cayenne pepper and oregano. Pour tofu cream sauce over it and heat slowly. Serve over soba noodles.

ROASTED BELL PEPPER

Cut peppers in half. Take out seeds. Roast over stove flame until black. Put into plastic bag, seal and refrigerate for 15 minutes. Take out of bag and wash peppers under cold water. Slice in medium size pieces.

SAUCE

1 pound soft tofu
1 cup soy milk
2 tablespoons oregano
1 teaspoon tamari
cayenne pepper, dash
1 tablespoon nutritional yeast
Mix all ingredients in blender.

NASI GORENG DE INDONESIA

This is what I ate when I was on Bali. It is a very simple dish, and it tasted the best freshly prepared at Ubud's funky market. By the way, Ubud's market is a great place to meet other travelers from all over the world.

2-4 cups cooked rice
1-2 tablespoons oil
1-2 onions, diced
1 bunch green onion
2-4 carrots, sliced
1-2 cloves garlic
1-2 tablespoons fresh ginger
1/2 teaspoon Sambal Olec, very hot
salt
eggs, optional

Sauté onions, green onions, garlic and ginger in oil. Add Sambal Olec, carrots and rice. Stir well, and sauté until the vegetables are done. Serve with a fried egg on top.

GADO GADO INDONESIA

This is another dish I ate when I was on Bali. It is a very simple dish, vegetables with a spicy peanut sauce.I always wanted to learn how to make a good peanut sauce. For years I had been making a peanut sauce that just did not seem quite right. So I brought this recipe back from Bali.

PEANUT SAUCE

2-3 cups raw Spanish peanuts
1/2 cup onion, minced
1-2 cloves garlic
1 tablespoon fresh ginger, minced
1/2-1 teaspoon Sambal Olec
salt, dash
1-2 cups water

Roast peanuts in baking oven at 375°F for about 5 minutes or until light brown. Let cool down and grind in food processor or blender. Sauté onions, garlic and ginger. Add peanuts, spices and water, stir well because it burns easily.

VEGETABLES

2-4 carrots
2-3 zucchini
1-2 bok choy
1-2 onions, diced

2 cloves garlic

Cut vegetables into medium size pieces. Sauté all vegetables in oil, starting with onions and garlic, then carrots, bok choy and at last zucchini. Serve with peanut sauce on top.

THAI CURRY

Sometimes, when I miss traveling, I just cook meals from foreign countries and imagine I am there. It is a great, short vacation.

> 1-2 tablespoons sesame oil
> 2-3 carrots
> mushrooms, some
> snow peas, some
> 1-3 zucchini
> 1-2 stems broccoli
> 1/4-1/2 head of cauliflower
> 1-2 onions
> 1-3 cloves garlic
> 1-2 tablespoons fresh ginger
> 1/4 teaspoon yellow curry paste, canned
> 1 can coconut milk
> 1 teaspoon curry powder, optional
> 1 bunch lemon grass
> salt

Start by preparing tea from the lemon grass. Cut lemon grass into a pitcher and pour boiling water over it. Cover and let sit for at least 15 minutes. Sauté the onions, garlic and ginger in sesame oil, add curry paste and stir well. Add mushrooms, then snow peas, followed by carrots, cauliflower and broccoli. Add lemon grass tea and let simmer until vegetables are almost done, now add zucchini, coconut milk and salt. If you want more sauce, use more lemon grass tea. Do not boil after adding coconut milk.

ENCHILASAGNA / ENCHILADAS

These dishes have the same base, the only difference being in how you put them into the pan. You can make individual rolls/enchiladas or spread it into the pan like lasagna/enchilasagna.

        12 corn tortillas
        1-2 tablespoons oil
        5 tomatoes, diced
        2 onions, diced
        garlic
        3 bell peppers, diced
        1/2-2 green chilies
        cilantro
        parsley
        2 cups tofu ricotta
        1 cup soy jalipeño cheese, grated
        1 cup soy mozzarella
        1-2 teaspoons arrowroot, optional
        1-2 teaspoons nutritional yeast
        salt
        cayenne, dash

Sauté onions and garlic for 5 minutes, then add tomatoes and bell peppers. Simmer until almost done. Add green chilies, parsley, cilantro, tofu ricotta, soy jalipeño cheese, and all spices. Stir well. If it is too soupy, mix arrowroot with some sauce and stir it back in. Simmer for 5 minutes more. For Enchilasagna: Heat oil in a skillet and fry the corn tortillas for a short moment. Layer an oiled baking pan with the tortillas (almost like a crust) and fill with the tomato mixture. Finish with a layer of tortillas. Cover with parchment paper and aluminum foil and bake for 20 minutes. Remove foil, sprinkle the top with soy mozzarella cheese. Bake for another 10 minutes. Let cool for 10-15 minutes before cutting. For Enchiladas: Heat oil in a skillet and fry the tortillas for a short moment. After removing tortillas from skillet, fill each with 2-3 tablespoons tomato mixture, roll them up and layer them into an oiled baking pan. Cover lightly with leftover tomato mixture, sprinkle with soy mozzarella cheese and bake for 15-20 minutes at 375°F.

INDIAN CURRY

2-4 tablespoons ghee or butter
1 teaspoon brown mustard seeds
1 teaspoon fenugreek

1 bay leaf
1 cinnamon stick
1 onion, diced
garlic, minced
1-2 teaspoons fresh ginger, minced
salt

2-4 teaspoons curry powder
1-2 teaspoons tomato paste
1-2 cups water

Vegetables (cut into medium size pieces)
　　　cauliflower
　　　snow peas
　　　carrots
　　　broccoli
　　　zucchini

mushrooms
red bell peppers
1/2-1 cup applesauce
1/2-1 cup tofu sour cream or yogurt

Sauté first group of ingredients until the seeds start to pop. Add second group of ingredients and let simmer until they are soft. Make a curry paste by mixing curry powder with a little water. Add curry paste and tomato paste to the onion. Stir well and then add the vegetables, starting with the ones taking longer to cook. This way the other ones will not overcook. Add 2 cups water, cover and simmer until vegetables are almost done. Add applesauce and yogurt. Stir well and simmer for 5 minutes more. Take out the cinnamon stick and the bay leaf. Serve with basmati rice, chutney, raita, coconut flakes and chapaties.

MUSHROOM TEMPEH STROGANOFF

1-2 packages tempeh, diced
1-2 tablespoons oil
2-3 onions, quartered
2 cloves garlic, minced
1-1 1/2 pounds mushrooms, whole
2 red bell peppers, diced
1/2 bunch parsley
1/2 teaspoon paprika
salt
pepper

First prepare the tempeh marinade and the tofu cream sauce. Sauté onions and garlic in oil for 5 minutes. Add bell peppers and mushrooms and sauté 5-8 minutes more. Season with salt, paprika and pepper. Pour tofu cream sauce over it and heat until hot. Do not boil. Mix in parsley and fried tempeh. Serve with pasta or brown rice.

    3 tablespoons tamari
    3-4 tablespoons water
    1 teaspoon lemon juice
    1/2 teaspoon yeast flakes
    drop honey
    cayenne pepper

Mix all ingredients together and marinate tempeh for at least 1/2 hour. Take tempeh out of marinade and fry in a little oil until light brown, then add to Stroganoff.

    1/2 pound soft tofu
    1-2 cups soy milk
    1-2 tablespoons tamari
    1 teaspoon paprika
    1-2 tablespoons yeast flakes
    dash of fresh or dried herbs: thyme, marjoram or oregano

Cream all ingredients in a blender. Start with 1 cup soy milk and 1 tablespoon tamari. Add more if necessary.

BROCCOLI WITH SESAME

Simple but delicious!

Sauté broccoli in ghee or in sesame oil until soft. Sprinkle toasted sesame seeds over broccoli. Serve with brown rice, tofu patties and a big salad.

RICE NUT LOAF
(4 - 6 servings)

2-3 onions, chopped
1-2 garlic cloves, diced
2 pounds mushrooms
3-4 carrots, grated
1 red bell pepper, diced
2 zucchini, diced
1/2 cup parsley
1 cup walnuts, toasted & ground
1 cup cashews, toasted & ground
4 cups brown rice, cooked
1 1/2 cups water & 1 1/2 teaspoons arrowroot
2-3 cups tofu ricotta
1 package soy cheese, grated
thyme, marjoram
salt, pepper

Sauté onions, garlic and mushrooms for about 10 minutes. Add bell peppers and zucchini and sauté for 5 minutes more. Put rice into a big bowl, add carrots, sautéed vegetables and all other ingredients. Spice with salt and pepper and mix well. Heat oven to 375°F. Oil baking dish and pour the mixture into it and press down. Bake for 1 hour or until top is brown.

GINGER CARROTS

If you are looking for an easy, fast and healthy meal try this one.

1/2 cup almonds
3/4 cup tamari
3/4 cup water
1 tablespoon ghee
8-10 carrots
2-3 tablespoons fresh ginger, grated
1 teaspoon dill
1-2 teaspoons tamari
1 teaspoon honey, optional

Soak almonds in tamari-water mixture for about 15 minutes then remove. Heat oven to 375°F and bake almonds for about 8 minutes or until light brown. (Cover bottom of baking pan with parchment paper, to keep it from burning.) Cut carrots into sticks. Heat ghee in wok, add ginger and carrots. Cover with lid. Sauté until carrots are done, stirring once in a while. Add tamari, dill and baked almonds. Drizzle honey over it and stir. Serve with quinoa and baked tofu.

LIFE WIND

Life is passing fast,
like the wind on our mountain.
A soft breeze, shaking up tension,
making trees talk and sing.
Hair getting wild, hanging in my eyes.
Wind touching my body,
crawling under my purple skirt,
touching my white lace panties.
Then quietness for a second,
before new wind grows
to this big blow.
What's happening in my life?
Stuckness gets blown away.
New times starting.
Body changes, menopause,
no moon, hotflashes,
heat everywhere.
Beauty, soft skin
wildness, emptiness.
Embracing my lover,
feeling laughter, stillness,
joy, slow motion.
Wind is blowing, whispering in my ear,
"Have patience."

BREADS

BREAD IS WONDERFUL TO MAKE. I know, it takes a long time, but still it is worth doing. I like to knead dough and put all my love into it. It is a great meditation, where the mind gets quiet and peaceful. Love and the ingredients you are using are the key for good bread. To make your own bread you need at least 3 hours. But remember: you still have time to do something else between the rising and baking. Very often I am asked what I think about bread machines; they are easy to use, less time consuming and after all the argument, they produce homemade, fresh bread. That is true. If the alternative is buying bread or making it in a machine, I would prefer using a machine. However, I think that machine-made bread is missing something very important and I would prefer to take the time to make it by hand. Bread made in a machine is just bread, but bread made by hand is bread with your personal touch and it has a different taste.

I personally like to get in a meditative space and create something that makes me feel good and has a wonderful taste. Making bread can be easy and it can be difficult. It is also very personal! There are many ways of doing it, and if you are talking to a bread baker, there is only one way, his or hers. So, here is my way, it works best for me, to create bread how I like it.

BASIC YEAST DOUGH
(makes 2 loaves)

3 cups whole wheat flour
2¹/2 cups unbleached white flour
2 packages active dry yeast (2 tablespoons)
1 drop honey
¹/2 cup warm water
¹/4 cup oil
2 teaspoons salt
1¹/2-2 cups warm water
¹/2 cup unbleached white flour for kneading

Use a medium size bowl so that it is easy for you to knead the dough and it has space to expand. Dough is pretty sensitive and does not like plastic bowls too much.

Mix 3 cups whole wheat and 2¹/2 cups white flour in your bowl. Make a well with your fist in the middle of the flour. Pour yeast, honey and ¹/2 cup warm water into the middle and use your finger to mix in some flour, to make a liquid paste. This is the sponge. Cover bowl with a towel and let the mixture sit for about 10 minutes in a warm place, to let the yeast rise.

Add oil, salt and 1¹/2 cups water to the sponge and mix first with a wooden spoon and then by hand. Mix well and start kneading. If the dough is too wet, add more flour, too dry add more water. The dough should be easy to work and not stick to the bowl. Knead for about 15 minutes then take out of the bowl, oil your bowl generously, and place the dough back in it. Move it around and turn it over, so that both sides of the dough are coated with oil. Cover the bowl with a towel and let the dough rise in a warm place (about 1 hour). Now is a good time to oil the loaf pans.

Punch dough down, flour your kneading surface, then let the dough slide onto it. Divide dough evenly in two parts. Now the fun part begins. Take a deep breath and enjoy kneading your bread dough. The dough likes to be touched, therefore kneading is very important. Do knead for at least 10 minutes with a conscious mind and love. You cannot overdo it. Shape the loaves and put into the oiled bread pans, score with knife, cover with a towel and let rise again for 30 minutes. Meanwhile heat oven to 375°F. Now the bread dough is ready to be baked. To get a crispy crust you can spray the bread with water after you have put it into the oven. Baking time varies. It takes between 35 and 50 minutes. Make sure to check after 35 minutes. To check bread you take it out of pan and hit the bottom. If it sounds hollow it is done, if not, continue baking. Sometimes the upper crust gets dark too fast. To prevent that cover the top with aluminum foil. When the bread is done and it looks just like you want it, let it cool for about 5 minutes in the loaf pan and then take it out and place it onto a cooling tray to get a nice crispy crust.

That's the basic dough. If you want to add something, like herbs, seeds, onion, garlic or whatever comes to your creative mind, add it after the sponge is ready, together with salt, oil and water.

You can give the bread different shapes. I like to make baguettes. You don't have to use the bread pans, but my experience is that the bread bakes nicer in one. You also can make rolls from all the following recipes. Do not oil the baking sheet, just sprinkle with cornmeal.

SUNFLOWER SEED BREAD

3 cups whole wheat flour
2 1/2 cups unbleached white flour
2 packages active dry yeast (2 tablespoons)
1 drop honey
1/2 cup warm water
1/2 cup oil
2 teaspoon salt
1 cup sunflower seeds
1 1/2-2 cups warm water

Follow the basic yeast dough recipe. Add the sunflower seeds with oil, salt and water, and continue with the recipe.

MULTI-GRAIN BREAD

1 1/2 cups whole wheat flour
2 cups unbleached white flour
2 packages active dry yeast (2 tablespoons)
1 drop honey
1/2 cup warm water
3/4 cup rolled oats
3/4 cup cracked wheat (soaked in boiling water)
1/2 cup millet
1/4 cup oil
2 teaspoons salt
1 1/2-2 cups warm water
1/2 cup white flour for kneading

Make a sponge out of the above ingredients and then go on with the basic yeast dough recipe. Soak the cracked wheat in 1 cup boiling water for about 15 minutes. Add millet, soaked cracked wheat and oats together with oil, salt and water to the sponge and continue with the recipe.

ITALIAN OREGANO BREAD

2 cups whole wheat flour
4 cups unbleached white flour
2 teaspoons active dry yeast
1 drop honey
1/2 cup water
1/4 cup oregano, fresh or dried
1/4 cup oil
2 teaspoons salt
2 cups water

Follow the basic recipe. If you want your bread lighter and fluffier, use less whole wheat and more white flour.

ONION BREAD

2 cups whole wheat flour
4 cups white flour
2 teaspoons active dry yeast
1 drop honey
1/2 cup water
13/4 cups onions (sliced in thin half moons)
1/4 cup oil
2 teaspoons salt
2 cups water

After you have prepared the sponge, sauté onions in oil until they are soft. Use low heat. Set aside to cool and follow the recipe.

INGRID'S QUICK BREAD
(makes 2 loaves)

One day, when I was cooking for a 16-day yoga retreat at the White Lotus Foundation, I needed bread for an Italian dinner. Unfortunately I had forgotten to start in time to make the bread I usually make. I was in big trouble. Then I remembered a recipe that a German girlfriend gave to me that I had refused to use. It takes much less time and that was just what I needed. I was very skeptical about that bread, but I have to say, everybody loved it. It also passed my critical judgment.

    2 cups whole wheat flour
    2 cups unbleached white flour
    4 tablespoons vinegar
    2 packages active dry yeast
    3 teaspoons salt
    2 cups sunflower seeds
    4 1/4 cups warm water

Mix all ingredients together and fill evenly in two oiled bread pans. Dough will be moist. It has no rising time! Put into unheated oven and bake at 375°F for about 60 minutes. When bread is done, cool for 5 minutes and then transfer onto cooling tray.

CORNBREAD
(makes 1 loaf)

    1/4 cup honey
    2 cups soy milk
    1/2 teaspoon arrowroot in 1/2 cup water
    6 tablespoons oil or melted butter
    2 cups cornmeal

2 cups whole wheat flour
4 teaspoons baking powder
1 teaspoon baking soda
1 teaspoon salt

Mix together honey, soy milk, water with arrowroot and melted butter or oil. Mix the flour, cornmeal, baking powder, baking soda and salt in a separate bowl. Add to the honey mixture and stir just enough to combine the two. Pour mixture into oiled pan and bake for 15-20 minutes or until top is light brown. Let cool for 5 minutes. Serve warm straight from pan. You also can change this recipe and add: corn (canned or fresh), soy cheese, sautéed onions, herbs, red pepper flakes, chili powder, or whatever you desire.

RAISIN BREAD

3 cups whole wheat flour
3 cups unbleached white flour
2 packages active dry yeast
1 drop honey
1/2 cup warm water
1/4 cup oil
2 cups honey
salt, dash
11/2-2 cups warm water
11/2 cups raisins
11/2 cups walnuts
4 teaspoons cinnamon

Make a sponge and let rise for 10 minutes. Then add all other ingredients and follow the basic recipe. Bake at 375°F

MENOPAUSE

I'm in menopause!
That is what I thought.
No menopause any more.
Menopause, coming and going,
Passing through.
Menopause—being old,
no sex—no lover.
The end of a road,
the end of being young.
That is what I thought,
when I was young.
Young, old—so what.
I'm wise and old and young.
Menopause lets me look to myself,
to my sisters.
Menopause—hot flushes.
No children any more—never?
Maybe tomorrow
maybe never—ever—always.
I like that page of my life book.
The page of wisdom and creativity.
Fly off to the red sky
and dance with the wise women.

MUFFINS

BANANA MUFFINS
(makes 8)

These muffins are made without dairy or eggs. They taste great.

1/4 cup soft tofu
1/3 teaspoon arrowroot dissolved in 1/3 cup water
1 teaspoon vanilla
1/3 cup oil
1/2 cup honey
3 bananas, mashed
1 cup whole wheat flour
1 cup pastry flour
1/4 cup oat bran, optional
2 teaspoons baking powder
1/2 teaspoon baking soda
1 teaspoon cinnamon
salt, dash

Mix the first five ingredients in blender. Pour into a bowl. Mash bananas with a fork and add to mix. Set aside. Mix all dry ingredients together. Set aside. Oil muffin tins or better if you use muffin paper cups in tins. Combine dry ingredients with banana mix. Stir only as long as necessary to combine. Using a tablespoon, fill muffin papers or tins 3/4 full. Bake for 15-20 minutes at 375°F. Let cool in tins for 5 minutes then transfer to cooling tray.

BLUEBERRY MUFFINS
(makes 8)

Use the same recipe as above, but substitute frozen blueberries for the bananas. Blueberries have more liquid, so use more arrowroot. 1 teaspoon arrowroot to 1/3 cup water then go on with the recipe.

These muffins are also great with steamed, mashed squash. You can also add raisins, walnuts, almonds, carob chips or let your imagination run wild.

WHOLE WHEAT BRAN MUFFINS
(makes 12)

1/4 cup oil
1/3 cup honey
1 1/2 cups soy milk
1/3 teaspoon arrowroot dissolved in 1/3 cup water
1 cup whole wheat flour
1 cup bran
2 teaspoons baking powder
salt, dash

Mix the first five ingredients together and set aside. Mix all dry ingredients, and combine with liquid mix. Oil muffin tins or use paper muffin cups in tins, and fill 3/4 full. Bake for 20 minutes at 375°F. Cool for 5 minutes, then transfer muffins to cooling tray.

Ceremonial Dance, 1994
Tempera on paper

BE 50

50, the age of beauty and wisdom.
Turn around.
See the path you came.
The path through
deserts, mountains and oceans.
Blue sky, dark clouds,
thunder and bright sun.
You traveled the path, out of the unknown
to the now,
the moment of your great being.
At 50 you know and
you don't.
That's what keeps you alive,
keeps life changing and moving.
That's when you fly off
and a new path is in front of you
unknown and full of excitement.
The path of your dreams.

PANCAKES &
FRENCH TOAST

OAT-BUTTERMILK PANCAKES
(Makes 8-12 pancakes)

If you want pancakes with the greatest taste, light and crispy outside, then try this recipe. Start the batter the night before, to help to soften the rolled oats.

> 2 cups rolled oats
> 2 cups buttermilk or
> soy milk with 1/2 teaspoon lemon juice
> 1/2 teaspoon arrowroot in 1/2 cup water
> 1/4 cup oil or butter melted and cooled
> 2 tablespoons honey
> 1/2 cup unbleached white flour
> 1 teaspoon each: baking powder and soda
> 1/2 teaspoon cinnamon
> salt, dash

In a bowl combine oats, buttermilk or soy milk with lemon juice. Mix well. Cover tightly and refrigerate overnight. Take out of refrigerator and just before frying, add arrowroot water, oil or butter and honey. Stir to blend. In a separate bowl mix all the dry ingredients and add to oat mixture. If batter seems too thick, add a little more soy milk or buttermilk. In a frying pan, lightly oiled and heated, pour as much batter as needed to get the size pancakes you want. Cook until top starts getting dry, but is still moist. Flip over and cook the other side until browned.

BANANA PANCAKES

You can use the same recipe as above. Cut bananas into the batter just before cooking.

CORN QUINOA PANCAKES
(Makes 6 pancakes)

Wheat and gluten-free pancakes! They taste really good.

> 1 cup corn meal
> 1 cup quinoa flour
> 1/4 cup water with 1 teaspoon arrowroot
> 1 banana, mashed
> 1 tablespoon lemon juice
> 1 teaspoon baking powder and soda
> 1/4 cup melted butter or oil

Mix all dry ingredients together. Add butter or oil, lemon juice, water with arrowroot, the banana and mix. If you can't find quinoa flour, make your own, grinding up quinoa in your blender.

FRENCH TOAST

This is an easy dish to prepare and good tasting.

8 slices whole wheat bread
1 block soft tofu
1/2 cup soy milk
4-6 tablespoons maple syrup
1/2 teaspoon cinnamon
1/2 teaspoon lemon juice

Place the bread into an oiled baking dish. Mix all other ingredients except cinnamon in blender. Add more maple syrup if desired. Pour evenly over bread. Sprinkle with cinnamon. Bake for about 15 minutes at 375°F.

DESSERTS

W E ALL LIKE THEM and we all fear them. Too much sugar, too many calories, too much fat. The list is long why we hesitate to enjoy desserts as much as we do other foods. I don't want to talk you into eating desserts, but if you can't resist, try one of these—low dairy, no sugar, no eggs!

STRAWBERRIES WITH VANILLA SAUCE

Strawberries
mint leaves
maple syrup

Wash strawberries, take leaves out, and cut into slices. Pour some maple syrup over them. Mix in the mint leaves and let sit at room temperature.

VANILLA SAUCE

1 cup almonds, blanched
2 cups soy milk
2 tablespoons vanilla
2-4 tablespoons maple syrup

To blanch the almonds, pour boiling water over them and let sit for 10 minutes. Now you can take off the skins very easily. Dry the almonds with a kitchen towel and then puree in blender. Add soy milk, maple syrup and vanilla. If the sauce is too thick add more soy milk.

BANANA ICE CREAM

Do you have a Champion juicer? If so, you can make the best ice cream. For this dessert you have to plan ahead. At least 3 days before you want to eat the ice cream you need to freeze ripe, peeled bananas. I normally use 1 banana per person, but if you like ice cream a lot it might not be enough. Put the frozen bananas through the juicer and where normally the pulp comes out, your ice cream appears. Serve it right away. Don't freeze it again, it will turn brown. Variation: Use frozen berries, mangos, grapes, etc. This way you can create beautifully colored ice cream.

NUT DATE BALLS

Easy, healthy and fast.

> 1/2 cup cashews
> 1/2 cup almonds
> 1/4 cup Brazil nuts, optional
> 1/2 cup dried figs
> 1 cup dates
> coconut flakes

Use food processor to grind up the nuts. Mush figs, dates and nuts together. Roll into little balls with wet hands and roll them in coconut flakes.

RICE-APRICOT PUDDING

> 1 cup dried apricots
> 3 cups brown rice, cooked
> 1 cup water
> 1 cup soy milk

1 cup honey
1 teaspoon lemon juice
1/2 cup soft tofu
1 teaspoon vanilla
2 tablespoons tahini, optional
1 cup almonds

Cover apricots with water and boil until soft. Stir once in a while. Mix all wet ingredients in blender. Cut up almonds by hand or in food processor. Mix all ingredients together and fill into oiled baking dish. Bake at 350°F for 1-1 1/2 hours or until top is light brown. Variation: Use millet instead of rice.

MOUSSE AU CHOCOLAT/CAROB

4 cups soy milk, rice dream or amazake
2 tablespoons kuzu
1 cup carob or chocolate chips
1 cup carob powder or cocoa
4 tablespoons maple syrup
1/2 teaspoon orange rind, optional

Heat 3 cups soy milk. Mix carob powder with remaining soy milk until smooth. Dissolve kuzu in a little water, add all ingredients to soy milk and boil once, then turn off the heat. Stir well! Add orange rind if desired. Let it cool down. Cover with plastic wrap and cool it overnight, or at least for 3 hours in the refrigerator. To make it more creamy mix it up in the blender.

TOFU-STRAWBERRY MOUSSE

    1 pound soft tofu
    2 baskets strawberries
    2-4 tablespoons maple syrup
    1 teaspoon vanilla

Wash the strawberries, take off the leaves and set one basket aside. Mix all ingredients in blender. Use more maple syrup if not sweet enough. Slice the leftover strawberries into a bowl and mix tofu mousse over them. Cover with plastic wrap and refrigerate for at least 3 hours.

MANGO-STRAWBERRY MOUSSE

This is a most sensual dessert.

    1 pound soft tofu
    1 mango
    2-4 tablespoons maple syrup
    1 teaspoon vanilla
    1 basket strawberries

Peel mango and cut off the meat. Put all ingredients except the strawberries into the blender and puree until smooth. Pour into a bowl. Slice strawberries and mix into mango mousse. Cover with plastic wrap and refrigerate for at least 3 hours.

ORANGE PEARS WITH CAROB SAUCE

4 pears
1/4-1/2 cup fresh orange juice
4-6 tablespoons maple syrup
cinnamon, dash

Heat oven to 375°F. Wash and core whole pears. Set them in a baking dish and pour orange juice and maple syrup into the hole and over pear. Sprinkle with cinnamon and bake for 15-20 minutes. In the meanwhile prepare the sauce. Set each pear on individual plate and drip carob sauce in a decorative way over pear and some onto the plate.

SAUCE

2-4 tablespoons carob powder or chips
2-4 tablespoons oil or ghee
2-3 tablespoons honey
2-3 teaspoons arrowroot dissolved in a little soy milk

Make a paste out of carob and a little soy milk. Heat oil, honey, carob paste and arrowroot. Stir constantly. Add more soy milk if sauce is too thick. Let boil once, then turn heat off. Instead of carob you can use chocolate chips or cocoa.

CAKES

CARROT CAKE

1 1/2 cups oil
1 cup honey
1 teaspoon arrowroot in 1 cup water
2 teaspoons vanilla
1-2 teaspoons lemon juice
2 cups carrots, grated
1 cup unbleached white flour
1 1/2 cups whole wheat flour
1 teaspoon salt
1/4 teaspoon baking soda
6 teaspoons baking powder
1 1/2 cups walnuts or almonds, coarsely chopped
1 teaspoon cinnamon
1/4 teaspoon allspice, optional

In a medium size bowl combine all dry ingredients. Mix well. In a big bowl mix oil and honey, then stir in arrowroot water, vanilla, lemon juice and carrots. Combine dry ingredients with carrot mixture and stir just enough to combine. Pour mixture into oiled cake pan and bake at 375°F for about 20 minutes or until cake is light brown and done. (Test with a toothpick. If it comes out clean, cake is done.) Take out of the oven and let it cool for 10 minutes, then flip cake over onto cooling tray and let cool completely. Now it is ready to be cut and served.

APPLE WALNUT CAKE

1¼ cups oil
1 cup honey
1 cup water with 2 teaspoons arrowroot
2 teaspoons vanilla
1-2 teaspoons lemon juice
4-5 apples, sliced
1 cup unbleached white flour
1½ cups whole wheat flour
1 teaspoon salt
¼ teaspoon baking soda
4 teaspoons baking powder
1 teaspoon cinnamon
1½ cups walnuts, coarsely chopped
½ cup raisins

Mix honey and other wet ingredients together and set aside. Combine all dry ingredients. Mix walnuts and raisins and set aside. Slice apples medium thick and drizzle lemon juice over them. Oil cake pan. Heat oven to 375°F. Combine the dry ingredients with the honey mixture and stir well but not too much. Cover the bottom of the baking pan with a thin layer of dough and smooth out with a rubber spatula. Layer apples on top of that. Sprinkle apples with walnut-raisin mixture and cover with a layer of dough. Bake for about 45 minutes. Check after 30 minutes. If the top gets too brown cover top loosely with aluminum foil. When cake is done, cool in pan for 15 minutes and then take out of pan and let it cool on rack.

HEAVENLY APRICOT BARS

These are my favorites and so easy to make.

1/2 bag dried apricots
1/2 cup whole wheat flour
1/2 teaspoon baking powder
salt, dash
1/4 cup butter, cold
1 teaspoon honey
2-3 tablespoons water
2 teaspoons oil

TOPPING

1/2 cup almonds, chopped
1 teaspoon vanilla
1 teaspoon arrowroot
2-3 tablespoons apple juice
2 teaspoons honey, optional

Cover apricots with water and cook them for about 20 minutes or until soft. Stir once in a while. Set aside to cool. Mix flour, baking powder and salt. Cut butter into little pieces and combine with flour mixture, using your finger tips. Combine honey, water and oil and pour slowly into flour/butter mixture to make a soft but not sticky dough. Oil cookie tray. Roll dough on floured surface, transfer to cookie tray and press it evenly onto the sheet with your hands. Take a fork and pierce some holes into the dough. Pre-bake at 375°F for 5-8 minutes. Let it cool. Use food processer to chop almonds. In a small bowl combine almonds, vanilla, arrowroot dissolved in apple juice and honey, mix well and let sit for 10 minutes. Use food processor to make apricot mousse out of cooked apricots. Fill into pre-baked dough and smooth out evenly. Cover with the almond topping.

Bake at 375°F for about 15 minutes or until top is light brown. Cool before cutting. Makes 6-8 bars.

PEACH COBBLER

4 cups peaches
2 tablespoons flour
1-2 tablespoons lemon juice
1/4 cup honey
1/2 teaspoon cinnamon

TOPPING

2 cups rolled oats
5 tablespoons oil or ghee, melted
3 tablespoons honey
1/2 teaspoon cinnamon
1/2 cup walnuts, chopped
1/4 cup flour
1/8-1/4 cup apple juice
salt, dash

Cut peaches into quarters and then into medium thick slices. Mix flour, lemon juice, honey and cinnamon with the sliced peaches and set aside. Oil a baking dish and fill the peaches into the bottom. Combine all ingredients for the topping and sprinkle on top of the peaches. Bake at 375°F for about 20 minutes. Serve hot or at room temperature. Variation: Mix blueberries and peaches. Use 1-2 tablespoons additional flour. For Apple Crisp: Follow the above recipe. Drip some lemon juice over apples, so that they do not turn brown. Use almonds instead of walnuts.

GERMAN PFLAUMEN KUCHEN

This is a unique German cake. I don't think I have eaten anything similar here in the States. It is almost like a pizza, with plums on top. Try it. Maybe you will like it as much as I do.

    3½ cups whole wheat pastry flour
    1 package active dry yeast
    1 drop honey
    ¼ cup apple juice
    ½ teaspoon salt
    2 teaspoons cinnamon
    ½ cup oil
    4 tablespoons honey
    1 teaspoon vanilla
    1 cup apple juice

Wash plums, cut in half and take out the pits. To make a yeast dough, you start by making a sponge (see section on bread making, page 100). Have flour ready in a medium size bowl. Make a well in the middle and pour yeast and honey into it. Use ¼ cup juice to mix yeast with honey and some flour. Cover with a towel and let sit in a warm place for 10 minutes. Add all other ingredients except apple juice. Add the juice slowly. Mix everything together and start kneading the dough. If you need more liquid, add more juice. You want an elastic, smooth dough. Oil the bowl and turn the dough over so that both sides are coated with oil. Cover with a towel and let rise in a warm place for about 1 hour. Oil baking tray. Punch dough down. Flour your work surface and roll dough out to fit onto your baking tray and cover its sides. Place dough on tray. Sprinkle a little arrowroot on top and put the plums face up in rows onto the dough. Put the plums close to each other, so that there are no big spaces. Sprinkle the top with brown sugar. Bake at 375°F for about 20 minutes or until dough is done.

TOFU-CHEESE FIG CAKE

A cheesecake without the cheese. Tofu is a great substitute.

2 pound soft tofu
1/4 cup oil
1/2 cup honey
1 tablespoon vanilla
1/4 teaspoon salt.
2-4 tablespoons lemon juice
8-10 figs, sliced
nut pie crust

Blend all first ingredients in blender. Pour the mixture into baked crust. Cover top with sliced figs. Bake for 30 to 40 minutes. Let cool and then refrigerate.

CRUST:

1/4 cup almonds, finely chopped
1/4 cup walnuts, finely chopped
1/4 cup butter, melted
1 tablespoon honey
1/2 teaspoon vanilla

Mix all ingredients for the crust together and press into oiled baking pan. Bake at 375°F for 4-5 minutes.

COOKIES

BROWNIES

$1/2$ cup oil
$1/2$ cup carob chips
1 cup water & 1 teaspoon arrowroot
$1/4$ teaspoon salt
1 cup honey
1 teaspoon vanilla
1 cup whole wheat flour
1 cup walnuts

Melt together oil and carob chips and let cool. Beat together the wet ingredients and combine the two. Fold in the flour and the nuts. Oil baking sheet, pour mixture onto it and smooth it evenly. Bake 375°F for about 25 minutes. Makes about 30 brownies. If you want the brownies richer and more fancy, make a carob icing and decorate each brownie with a walnut half. You also can substitute chocolate for carob.

ICING

$1/2$ cup carob chips
$1/4$ cup soy milk
1 teaspoon kuzu
2 tablespoons honey

Melt together soy milk, honey and carob chips. Dissolve kuzu in a little water and add to carob mixture. Stir well and bring to a boil. Let it cool for a moment and then it is ready to use. Enjoy this healthy version of a brownie.

OAT CHEWS

1 cup oil
2 cups honey
3/4 cup soy milk
2 teaspoons vanilla
4 cups oats
3 1/4 cups whole wheat flour
1 teaspoon baking soda
1 teaspoon cinnamon
1/2 teaspoon salt
1 cup raisins

Mix wet ingredients together and set aside. Mix dry ingredients together and combine the two. With a tablespoon drop dough onto a cookie sheet and flatten out with a fork. Leave some space between each cookie. Do not oil the cookie sheet. Bake at 375°F for 10 minutes or until light brown. Makes about 10 big cookies.

GINGER SNAPS

1/2 cup oil
3/4 cup molasses
1/2 cup honey
1/4 cup water & 1/4 teaspoon arrowroot
2 cups whole wheat flour
2 teaspoons baking soda
1/2 cup wheat germ
3 tablespoons fresh ginger, grated

Mix dry and wet ingredients in separate bowls and then combine the two, stirring well. Spread a thin layer onto an ungreased cookie sheet and bake for about 10 minutes or until brown. Let cool for 5 minutes and then cut into squares or triangles. Serve with Yogi tea. Makes about 24 cookies.

WISE WOMAN

Wise woman
was sitting on a rock,
her feet touching
mother earth.
Listening to the sound
of the ocean.
She knew,
that she had found
her place,
that there was no need
to fill the space.
Only to listen, to be still
and to dive into surrender.
She could trust
her Inner Knowing.

Red Flower, 1993
Tempera on paper

SUFI STORY

Many years ago I read this story. I don't remember the author or the book title. What I remember is that this story had a big impact on my life.

I had been a vegetarian for maybe one year. I thought that being very strict and rigid would be the only way of being a true vegetarian. I never ate anything that had been in touch with meat and I have to admit that I also judged people who still were eating meat. Then I read this story:

A young woman, on her spiritual quest, was looking for this one teacher, not knowing where she could find him. It happened that she met a man who knew this teacher. He invited her to a gathering, where she could get in touch with him. She was excited and thankful for the invitation and went to the gathering.

She was surprised to see a table full of beautiful foods. From a lot to a little bit, some meat, fish, vegetables, fruit and also wine. She expressed her discomfort about all this food and let people know how easy it was for her to live on five oranges a day and how healthy and vital she felt. She walked around and talked to many people and told them her belief.

The gathering was coming to an end and she still had not met the teacher she was looking for. Asking the man who had invited her to this place where the teacher was, he answered, "You missed him because you were so busy talking about your five oranges."

I saw myself in this woman. Being judgmental, not flexible, I realized that I missed opportunities. I remember times when friends invited me to dinner and I heard myself saying, "Oh thank you, but I do not eat meat. I am vegetarian." I did not appreciate the food and the work—I was only concerned about being vegetarian. Also living in Mexico taught me to be more open and thankful for invitations to meals. It would have been not respectful on my side to refuse a meal that had been prepared especially for me. Since I read this story, many years have passed by. I am still vegetarian, but my tunnel vision has disappeared. It was a great lesson I received from this story.

MENU IDEAS

I HEAR A LOT FROM PEOPLE about how much they like to cook, but that they just don't have the time to browse through cookbooks to get fresh and inventive ideas to create their menus. Here are some of my favorite meals.

1. MIDDLE EASTERN STUFFED ZUCCHINI
Quinoa
Sunflower Seed Bread
Green Salad
Apricot Bars

Leftover stuffed zucchini make a delicious soup. Sauté some carrots, celery and onion. Add water and let simmer until vegetables are almost soft. Puree stuffed zucchini in blender and add to soup. Add tamari if desired.

2. MEXICAN DINNER
Black Beans
Rice
Guacamole
Salsa
Tortillas
Salad
Strawberry Mousse

If you have black beans left over, reuse them in a Spicy Black Bean Salad.

3. TARRAGON VEGETABLE CASSEROLE
Brown Rice
Baked Tofu
Carrot Cake

4. LASAGNA
Salad with cherry tomatoes, olives and sunflower sprouts
Baguette
Banana Ice cream or
Strawberries with Mint and Vanilla sauce

5. GADO GADO
Nasigoreng
Brown Rice
Salad
Oat Chews

6. LENTIL POTATO CASSEROLE
Tomato Soup
German Beet Salad
Orange Pears with Carob Sauce

7. INDIAN CURRY
Basmati Rice
Pear Orange Chutney
Raita
Chapatis
Nut Date Balls

8. PASTA POMODORE
Soba Noodles
Herb Baguette
Mixed Garden Salad
Mango Mousse

AFTERWORD

HERE YOU HAVE IT: a culmination of my learning, teaching and experience in the art of cooking—the art of taste. Initially, my work on this book was inspired by those of you who have tasted my food and asked for my recipes. I hope that sharing with you what I have learned will provide you with the incentive to use these recipes as "maps" in forging ahead to create your own unique style of cooking and preparing food. For those readers who may be new to vegetarian cooking or to my suggestions for alternative ways of looking at food preparation, I hope this book will inspire you to explore this world further. I have found that while I am always learning from others, I gain much of my insight from trusting my own intuition and experimenting with the unknown.

And finally, I would welcome and appreciate any comments, feedback and questions you have. You may write me at:

GOURMET CREATIONS
POST OFFICE BOX 41136
SANTA BARBARA, CALIFORNIA 93140